STORY WORKOUT

Also by Elisabeth Nonas

Non-fiction

City of Friends: A Portrait of the Gay and Lesbian Community in America (co-author with Simon LeVay)

Novels

Staying Home

A Room Full of Women

For Keeps

Story Workout:

Exercises to Help You Connect to the Stories You Want to Tell

By Elisabeth Nonas

Copyright © 2016 Elisabeth Nonas

All rights reserved. No part of this book may be reproduced or transmitted in any form or by any means, electronic or mechanical, including photocopying, recording, or by any information storage and retrieval system without the written permission of the author, except where permitted by law.

ISBN-13: 978-1533696137
ISBN-10: 1533696136
ASIN: B01HAJOJZA

www.elisabethnonas.com
Book design by Katherine Malcuria

DEDICATION

I wrote this book for you. Whether you're in a writing group, a class, or on your own, whether you already know the story you want to tell or just know that you want to tell stories. Even if you've already written a lot of stories and the title piqued your interest, I wrote this book for you. I hope it helps you find and nourish the connection between you and your stories.

ACKNOWLEDGMENTS

Thank you to Sharon Gedan and Sherry Thomas, who each read an early draft of this book and encouraged me to continue.

And also to Brennan Banta, who did some preliminary research for me when I was considering putting my thoughts about writing into a book.

My students have inspired me with their excitement for their stories. Working with them forced me to think deeply not only about how exactly we do what we do—get our stories onto the page—but also how to talk to them about the process and distill what I believe to be its essence into these chapters.

I couldn't have written this book without the love and support of Nancy K. Bereano, my firebrand.

TABLE OF CONTENTS

1. INTRODUCTION
Story notebook
Goals
Media history

2. INTERMISSION

3. INSPIRATION WILL FAIL YOU
Creative process

4. BELIEVE IN YOURSELF
Self-introduction

5. TRUST YOUR INSTINCTS

6. TAKE RISKS
Speaker response
Media responses
1. TV show ancillary content
2. Narrative videogames
3. Art/socially responsible video games
4. Adaptation
5. Transmedia

7. IT'S ALL IN THE DETAILS
Conflict
Building a story/story world
1. Preparation
2. Construction
3. Dissecting a story
4. Research

8. TRUTH VS. FICTION
What I heard
What I saw

9. IT'S NOT ABOUT THE RULES
Your rules

10. EVERYONE'S A CRITIC

11. CONCLUSION
One project
Story (re)defined
Goals revisited

12. THE END
Appendix A: On Constructive Criticism/ Giving
Appendix B: On Constructive Criticism/ Receiving

1 INTRODUCTION

The world doesn't need another book about writing. So why did I write it?

Nothing beats a good story. Doesn't matter if it's your favorite book or movie, video game or comic, or just your best friend telling you about her visit to her uncle's the time she and her cousin…when the cat climbed up the roof…the car ran out of gas…all the fuses blew…the purple shirt got mixed in with the white laundry…this extraordinary thing happened. And then… and then… and then… until finally….

Did you construct a story around each of those events? Probably. That's what we do.

We imagine the story as it's told to us, and we eagerly await the punch line: "That's why I don't eat plums." "They never spoke to each other again." "I found it in my desk, right where it was supposed to be all along."

We're invited to tell stories every day of our lives, only we don't always call them that. "Hey, how was your weekend?" "What'd you guys do last night?" "How did you two meet?"

Story is how we communicate. We explain, defend, propose. To a teacher, how we arrived at that answer; our position to a colleague or supervisor; a new idea to our team.

Many of us grapple with story outright. We write short stories or long (novels, novellas, creative nonfiction, articles), screen- and teleplays. Develop ideas for graphic novels, advertising campaigns, video games. Write proposals. We take photographs, make paintings and sculpture to express ourselves.

I have been teaching writing for over twenty years. Writing for longer. But it wasn't until a few years ago that I formally acknowledged to myself that a large part of what I was doing, beyond teaching about format and structure and language and tone, was trying to help students connect with the stories they wanted to tell.

When I first started teaching, I was the one with experience in various professional realms—I'd written screen- and teleplays, published novels and short stories, magazine articles. I had experience in pitch meetings, more than a few rejections from network and studio executives, writing for hire, as well as small and university press publication.

In addition to being the one who taught my students about proper script format and the "rules" of screenwriting, I felt my role to be one of mentor, encourager. We talked about process as well as themes, ideas, through lines, and three-act structure.

Spring 2006 changed all that, even if I didn't realize it at the time. In my senior capstone screenwriting course, three of my twelve students were serious video gamers. Two wrote screenplay adaptations of video game storylines. One student prepared me a detailed report about the different genres of games, as well as which companies were producing what kinds of games. I learned acronyms like FPS, RTS, RPG, ARG, as well as a host of new-to-me terms like boss battles, even a new definition of Easter eggs. Most importantly, I learned how many people were engaging in story in ways I hadn't understood until then.

Those students introduced me to realms I wasn't familiar with, hadn't been professionally active in. Now I own game consoles, have attended the Austin Game Developers Conference, the E3 Expo, and other professional and academic conferences centered on games and new and emerging media. While I can't say I'm an avid or even particularly competent gamer, those experiences reshaped my thinking about what it means to be a teacher meaningfully preparing my students for the professional world they will be entering—radically different from the one I had known. Together we have explored web series, video games, iPad apps (stand alone and some generated from fiction), alternate reality games, augmented reality. Not to mention slam poetry, medical case histories, painting and sculpture, graphic novels, regular old novels, advertising, myths, legends, and fairytales. I'm very interested in immersive narrative and immersive worlds and, for example, have received grants to study Disneyland as Story.

By now you're wondering what this has to do with why I wrote this book. It's all part of the story.

That initial exposure to various types of video games expanded my understanding of the professional world my students will enter, expanded my notion of the options of the kinds of stories they might have the opportunity to tell. Which dramatically altered how I thought I needed to prepare them to enter both the existing as well as the constantly evolving world of narrative delivery. I became convinced that the key to their future success lay in guiding them to the stories they want to tell and having that be the connection to the media they choose to work in. This rather than merely teaching them basic three-act structure and proper screenwriting format. Every professional I spoke with talked about needing good stories—no matter how much technology changes, whether game or app or new television show—everything starts with a story. I realized that if I arm my students with a solid understanding of what makes a good story, they will be able to apply that knowledge to existing forms as well as be prepared to write in new/emerging forms—or perhaps develop new forms themselves. That's why I believe story is key.

And that's why I wrote this book: to provide you with the same tools I provide my students in order to help you connect with the stories you want to tell.

What makes this book different from others is what it isn't: it's not about the rules you need to learn before you break them, the ten or three or five easy steps to writing the (your-genre-here) novel or screenplay. It isn't about how to make millions selling what you've written. Plenty of books and websites and seminars already exist to help you there.

So then what is the goal of this book? To encourage you to think about your own lives, the kinds of stories you relate to, how they make you feel, and how those feelings relate to the effect you want your stories to have on your audience. Discovering what connects you to these stories will enable you to articulate what you need to connect with in your own stories.

This is not a self-help book. This is a book of exercises designed to teach you to trust your instincts as a storyteller.

By writing about what informs/transforms your lives, you will make connections to a vast store of incidents and characters from which you can draw. If you were to examine—and you will have by the time you've completed these exercises—the themes of the books, films, television shows, and games you gravitate toward, you would see that's where the commonalities lie: love conquers all, power corrupts, honesty is the best policy. While the themes may be the same, it's the other parts—characters, dialogue, writerly and visual style, i.e., their creator's unique take on the common experience and their connection to their material—that give stories their individual voice.

I don't want to spend too much more time talking to you here. What I have to say is less important than what you need to tell yourself.

HOW TO USE THIS BOOK

Story Workout is devoted to helping you find and connect with the stories you want to tell. I conceived it as a renewable resource because writing isn't something you learn once and are done with. In my experience, it becomes both easier and harder the more you work at it. When I first started, it was enough for me to get a story onto the page. The more I wrote, the greater my technical facility. Need dialogue—I can write that. Some description—here you go. Easier and easier. However, as I developed my practice, my stories and themes became more complex. Which made articulating them more challenging. In addition, as my technical skills developed, so did my critical chops. I'd read what I wrote and see the gap between what I'd envisioned and what was coming out on the page, which meant more revising until the gap narrowed to a sliver (it rarely disappears completely). I tell my students that we're all after the same thing—a good story—and that the only difference between us as writers is that I've been working at it since before they were born.

I've assigned you seventeen exercises. I had a hard time determining their order. You could skip around, though I do recommend doing the first three first since they're the foundation upon which the others build. After that, you could go in order or as the exercises strike your fancy or are useful to what you're working on. When I was determining the sequence, I moved them around a lot. How can you talk about inspiration failing people before you've given them the hope of a practice of work?

What I'm offering here is a way to connect to your material. Sometimes by engaging directly with it. Other times by articulating for yourself what you're drawn to and why. Once you've gotten started, I will talk more about this idea of connection and why I think it's so crucial. I suggest you think about your audience and how you want to affect them based on how your favorite—or least favorite—works affect you. Maybe you're stuck, maybe you're just starting a new story or your first story (Welcome!).

I could have called this book *Story Workout: A Choose Your Own Adventure Book*. I didn't, but that, in effect, is what it is.

We all have stories to tell. I hope this book helps you connect to yours.

EXERCISE | STORY NOTEBOOK

Even if you already keep a journal or diary, start and maintain a separate story notebook.

Think of it as your repository for whatever strikes you as you're working through these exercises. In it, you may write, draw, paste articles or photographs, sketches for ideas, thoughts about speakers you've heard, movies you've seen, books you've read, snippets of dialogue you caught while waiting on line at the supermarket, your response to games you've played—any kind of story you've experienced. Have an idea for a story? Jot it down. Did a name for a character pop into your head? Put it in your notebook.

As you complete an exercise, return to the notebook to keep track of where you find inspiration, new ideas you might have for projects, or just to peruse what you've already written to use in one of the exercises.

If you're progressing through these exercises in a writing group or a class, you might schedule a time to meet every so often and use the material in your notebooks as a springboard for group discussions or sharing of new material.

EXERCISE | GOALS

Answer the following questions in your notebook:

- What is my creative goal?
- What do I hope to have accomplished when I've worked through all the exercises?
- What is my deadline to reach this goal?

Why: The more realistic you make your goal, the easier time you will have achieving it. Do you want to write your first story? Novel? A memoir? Develop an idea for a video game? Or start on your fourth story but aren't sure what it's really about?

Having a realistic goal doesn't mean you shouldn't push yourself, but don't plan on finishing your screenplay in two months if you've never written one before, don't know your idea, and have other time commitments (a job, a family, a full course load). Be honest with yourself.

Can your goal be broken into smaller milestones that will lead to the ultimate goal? For example, if you want to write a novel, what are some of the smaller steps you need to take to achieve that? Having a working title always helps me because my theme sometimes hides out there, and if I get stuck, looking at the working title reminds me what my story's about. I also need to lay out the plot from beginning to end. Not in great detail, but it helps me to know where I'm aiming to end up when I start out. I've been doing this for a lot of years now, so I'm pretty good at estimating the amount of time I need for each stage of a project. If I see I'm way behind, or ahead even, I can always recalculate.

Now, what helps me may not help you. (See: Inspiration Will Fail You, Believe in Yourself, Trust Your Instincts.) This is where you need to be honest with yourself. You're setting a series of attainable goals here so that you'll achieve your ultimate goal. And once that's set, you can go about preparations to attain it.

EXERCISE | MEDIA HISTORY

In your story notebook, make a list of what you respond to in media, what you like, and why. You don't need to list every single movie, game, book, television show, etc.; representative genres and styles with an example or two is fine.

Your list should include:

- What you watch—whether that's in a movie theatre, on television, your computer, live theatre, tablet, or phone;
- What you read (books, magazines, journals, blogs, scripts, plays, poems, comics, graphic novels, etc.);
- What video games you play (and it's okay if you don't play any); what your friends/family play (if they do);
- What you listen to (music, spoken word, talk radio);
- Any websites, virtual worlds, social media you spend time in.

After you've done that—Stop. I mean it. Stop. Don't read further until after you've made your lists.

Once you've finished your media history, look it over. See any patterns? Are you a sucker for tear-jerkers? Rom-com? Action? Do you go for deep character studies across all platforms, or only in novels? Do you go to movies for one kind of story, read novels for another? Or are you eclectic across the board? Any surprises? Any common links? If there are, jot them down in your notebook.

Do the stories you want to tell relate in some way to those you're drawn to read/watch/play? I ask because I believe that if you're not interested in the story you're telling—and by interested I mean so passionate about it that it doesn't let you rest—you can be sure your audience won't be, either. They can tell.

A note: I'm talking here about projects that you write because you want to write them, not because someone has hired you to write. I caution my students the same way. Don't write a story like (insert current blockbuster here) if that's not the kind of story you're interested in. Why, unless someone was paying you a hefty sum (plus benefits) to do so, would you want to spend your creative time and energy working on something just because you think it's what sells if it doesn't move you in some way?

My point is this: writing is hard work. Write what you want to write and what you care deeply about. Write want you want to read, see, play.

If you're doing these exercises in a group, sharing your media histories is a great way to get to know each other, learn who might have the same tastes as you, who might become a potential trusted reader/ sounding board for your ideas.

INTERMISSION

So much for the first three exercises that I hope you worked in order. From now on, feel free to progress numerically or as inspiration strikes (more on inspiration in a moment). I'll continue to describe each exercise, then explain why I think it's important. Every so often, I'll interrupt the exercises with some notes on writing.

Remember: you can always look back to check your goals, add to your timetable, remind yourself why you undertook this in the first place.

Ready? Take a deep breath. Off you go.

3
INSPIRATION WILL FAIL YOU

Being struck by a great idea is a beautiful thing. Being inspired to write a chapter, paragraph, scene, haiku, is fantastic. Getting that shot of adrenaline that comes with inspiration is better than many kinds of highs, legal or not. Losing yourself in a productive frenzy because of that inspiration—well, few experiences can match it.

But after you've spent those few hours before anyone was awake, or after everyone has gone to bed, or during an afternoon, or on a long plane ride when the words flowed and thoughts tumbled out and characters rushed onto the page or screen, after you've stowed your writing gear, gone back to the rest of your life, knowing for sure you'll come back to this because you're so inspired to work on it, what happens?

If you're like me, once the first flush of inspiration has faded, doubt sets in. You were all ready to tackle this terrific new idea, to let it take over and carry you away. But it's not the same now. The idea isn't a surprise anymore, it isn't overtaking you and forcing its way out through your fingers. In fact, maybe it isn't even such a good idea. Maybe the characters are derivative, you've read/seen this kind of story—no, this *very* story—a million times, nothing is fresh or different and isn't that the phone? Or a ping from Facebook? No stopping the voice in your head now: I've got bills to pay, errands to run, a job that demands my attention. Did I feed the dog? I'm only a student—what do I know? Guess this isn't a good time for me to write after all. I'll wait for that next flash of inspiration.

Here's the thing: inspiration will fail you. It's a boon when it strikes, but it won't always strike and it definitely won't last. I guarantee it. You can't simply wait for that to happen so you can continue this story/script/poem/project flush with the same excitement.

Which is why you need a practice. What do I mean by that? The better you understand your writing process, the better you'll be able to nurture it. Can you answer the following: What are your optimal working conditions? Do you have a routine? Or, if you don't have one, what would you like your routine to be?

Your practice may not look like my practice. Or your mentor's. Or your rival's. Or whatever favorite creative person's blog you follow. The important thing is to have that practice, to know and understand that…you can't start work in the afternoons or can only work in the afternoons, must have silence. Or music. Or scented candles.

Even then, not every writing session will be great. Sometimes the thoughts don't come. Dialogue is wooden and all text, no subtext. The connections you thought you had to your characters seem nonexistent. Which is understandable, because at this particular writing session you've realized that your characters are stupid and what made you think this was something you wanted to write anyway? Even in the midst of a rant like that, sometimes like Tinker Bell calling out to Peter Pan for help, your little idea flickers in your brain to remind you it's not dead yet. You don't care, of course, because you're done and are ready to tackle whatever task you've put off forever. Nothing like the thought of writing to inspire some writers to clean the kitchen or bathroom, do homework, anything rather than write. Perhaps you've heard the saying, "Writers love having written."

Whether or not that is the case for you, you will have days when the thoughts don't flow, the words are stuck in some goopy clay out of which they will not be pried or molded, and you wonder what the point is. This is especially true if you're not writing for an outside deadline, if no one is waiting for your story. For example, many times writing this book I wondered why I was doing it. What was the point of bringing another book on writing into the world. I don't know if I can satisfactorily answer that question other than to say I just needed to write it. I needed a place to put all the experiences I'd had with my own and my students' writing, and with the ways delivery of story is expanding. Basically, I couldn't *not* write this book.

So what did I do when I wasn't inspired to get to work? I worked on it anyway. Okay. Sometimes I cleaned my office. Or played backgammon on the iPad. But here we are, so I must have pushed through more often than not on the days when it wasn't easy.

That's what a practice can do for you. Enable you to work when you don't feel inspired.

I've learned over the years that I write best in the morning. That no matter how excited I am or engrossed in the story I'm creating, I can only make notes if I try to start mid-afternoon or at night. That sometimes taking a walk to explore a location I'm writing about will help me get unstuck. That's part of my process. Now, it took a while to have this lesson sink in, to understand the difference between when I needed to sit at my desk and hammer through to the other side of some wall between me and my story, and when I needed to step away from the computer and do something else.

Writing can take different forms—it isn't always actively writing. Most of it is—and that's hours slogging away, writing pages, editing pages, deleting pages, revising again. And again. But sometimes writing doesn't look like writing. It might be going to a museum, or a for a run, reading the paper. Sitting quietly. That all counts. Everything we do is grist for the mill and will turn up somewhere in our stories. And our stories progress even when we aren't actively working on them. Have you ever taken an extended break from something you were working on and when you returned to it, found it had different ideas on where it was going next? Not yet? Well, keep up your practice and you'll see what I'm talking about.

🔖 **The Lesson: You need a practice.**

EXERCISE | CREATIVE PROCESS, OR LOCATION, LOCATION, LOCATION

Real estate agents often spiff up a house when they put it on the market: a fresh coat of paint, flowers strategically placed, and rooms de-cluttered. They call it staging.

I once read an interview with Gabriel García Márquez in which he talked about taking very long showers in the morning because that was where he started to think about his writing for the day, and also about what he was going to wear: how he would dress for that day's work. Not everyone creates in old sweats and a t-shirt.

That's a kind of staging.

What about you? Where do you write? Or edit, think, process? Do you need absolute silence or white noise? Clutter, or a pristine space? A window out of which to gaze, or a blank wall onto which you project your stories? Some might believe that a cluttered workspace results in a cluttered mind. But maybe the piles of books or magazines, your notebooks, splayed out manuscript pages, maybe that's like white noise and precisely what you need to be productive. Or maybe you just need a good pair of headphones and a playlist to convert wherever you are—a crowded coffee shop, or park bench—into your ideal workspace.

Part of your creative practice will be figuring out what your process is. Some people can work anywhere. Some. Not all. Again, don't compare yourself. But do experiment for yourself.

Experiment with tools, also. Computer, tablet, pen and paper. Fountain pen? Ballpoint? Gel ink? Pencil? I personally love the sound of a fountain pen nib whispering across a page of good paper. But sometimes I need the speed I can only achieve typing on a computer. Whatever your preference, invest in the best you can afford, or whatever gives you pleasure, and enjoy the results.

Find your ideal writing space and decorate it with whatever is most conducive to your imagination. Or leave it bare and spare. The important message is: Don't shortchange yourself when it comes to your tools or your workspace.

Write brief responses to the following prompts.
Give yourself plenty of room in your notebook. And be honest!

- My ideal writing routine is to…
- How much can I deviate from this pattern and still be productive?
- My best times to work are…
- My least productive times are…
- Does this hold true at every stage of a project (inception, editing, proofreading)?

I like to work:
- In complete silence
- In a café surrounded by people
- Listening to music
- At a desk
- In a chair
- All of the above
- Other

I write best:
- On a computer
- On a tablet
- By hand

Add your own prompts to that list. Give serious thought to whatever you might need to create your optimal conditions and process.

Have you included your work habits, what you might like to change about them? If you don't already know what works for you, experiment with some different environments, methods, and conditions. Keep track of the results so you'll remember when you're stuck at some point later on (and yes, you will be) that you have a practice that can see you through the slow spots when inspiration fails you. If you've been slogging away unproductively, is it time to try working in a different space? Or do you need a bigger break? Is it time to go for a walk, to a museum, get some exercise to clear your head? Location isn't important only in real estate.

▌ The Lesson: The better you understand your writing process, the better you'll be able to nurture it.

4
BELIEVE IN YOURSELF

One night in Los Angeles in the late 70s I had dinner at a Thai restaurant on Sunset Boulevard. Seated near our table was a young guy (let's call him The Writer) and an older guy (let's call him The Producer). After a few minutes of small talk The Producer said, "So, let's hear your idea." At which point The Writer launched into a harrowing tale that landed his hero into every war currently raging on the planet. Different wars than we have now, but still plenty of hot-spots—Northern Ireland, the Middle East, you get the picture.

Personally, it sounded pretty dreadful to me, no real character development or purpose, just this endless war saga. But that's not the point.

When The Writer finally finished, he pushed himself back from the table and said, "And that's my story."

"Sounds like something Hemingway would write," said The Producer. The Writer didn't miss a beat: "That's exactly how I write."

All these years later I can still hear that. And his tone—kind of funny-you-should-mention-it-as-a-matter-of-fact-everyone-tells-me-that. Well, I can just about guarantee that he did *not* write like Ernest Hemingway.

I have no idea who The Writer was, or The Producer, if he even was a producer, whether or not that awful-sounding story ever got made, optioned, or even written. Whether he wrote like Hemingway was not the point. The point I want to make here is that The Writer did not miss a beat. He did not say, "Oh gosh, I wish I could write like that."

The Writer stood up for himself and his own work because no matter how much someone else likes it, no matter how much someone else believes in your work, no one's going to believe in it if you don't believe in it first. Especially when you're just starting out. No one's going to fight for it the way you will. No one's going to care about it as much as you do. You don't have to lie about it and say you write like Ernest Hemingway if you don't, but you do have to display unshakeable faith in it and in yourself.

And, unless you're getting paid to write someone else's story (and even there it helps to find your own connection to the material), you won't be able to believe in it if you haven't written something you were passionate about, that you needed to say. Upcoming lessons will help you discover what that connection is, but this is the deceptively simple lesson for now.

🔖 **The lesson: Write what you're passionate about.**

EXERCISE | SELF-INTRODUCTION

These first three exercises are about you—to get you thinking about the kind of media you consume (your media history), your response to it (story notebooks and media reports), your creative process, and, for this one, how your life to date has shaped you and, as a result, the stories you tell or want to tell.

The Exercise: Write an introduction of yourself. Incorporate these prompts:

- Two or three things that have informed and/or transformed your life. These "things" could be people, locations, situations, etc., anything that had a big impact on you.
- Themes you are drawn to. You can refer back to your media history to see what you wrote there.
- The effect you'd like your work to have on your audience.

Why: In addition to continuing the process of getting to know yourself (and/or each other if you're working in a group), think of this exercise as a prelude to your exploration of truth and fiction. (See: Truth vs. Fiction.)

There are a couple of ways you could do this exercise. If you're working on your own, write it out in your notebook and use it as source material later on.

If you know someone to share this with, do so following these guidelines: Beforehand, set a time limit for how long each person may speak. Three minutes is a good amount. Don't take longer than five. Make notes in your notebook on what you want to say. Practice so that you don't run over your time and can just glance at your notes and look up to actually connect with your group/audience rather than simply read what you've written.

5
TRUST YOUR INSTINCTS

We've all been told "write what you know." What does that mean? That our subject matter as writers is limited by our circumstances and what we've experienced? Limited also by what exists? Really? That would leave us with precious little to say. Or to read, for that matter.

So what does "write what you know" mean for us as storytellers? Think about it this way: Wherever our stories are set, whether in ninth-grade English class or on one of the sixty-odd moons of Saturn, whoever our characters are, what else are we writing but what we know? Whether we write about existing or fictional planets, whether our protagonists are human, animal, fairy, gnome, troll, elf, ogre, even if they're creatures from outer space, we write what we know about relationships, about people, about experiences we've had, that we've witnessed. We extrapolate from those experiences and we write.

"What we know" has come out of what we've observed and what we connected with but isn't limited to what actually exists.

A lot of the undergraduate student work I've read over the years has clearly been influenced by what these young writers have seen in movies and on television. Nothing wrong with that. But it isn't entirely right, either. Or not always right.

Too often we think our lives haven't been interesting enough, we haven't done enough, or certainly nothing "important" enough to write about. But one little kernel of experience can transform into an enchanted world or a space odyssey, an epic battle or an intimate family drama.

When I first started writing, I was trying to sell scripts or ideas for scripts. I kept trying to tell stories other people would be interested in because I didn't know the stories I wanted to tell. I was too inexperienced to understand what my work really lacked: a deep connection to my material.

What had first interested people in my writing was my connection to the sample screenplay I'd written, though I didn't really understand this at the time. No one ever articulated that to me, but if I think back on some of the earliest scripts I wrote, if I compare those ideas to what my students write, I recognize the similarities. If you'd asked me why I'd developed a particular idea, I'd probably have said because I thought I could sell it. I was turning in stories that looked like what I was seeing on television or in films.

And while I could write well enough, I didn't have much luck selling anything.

That made me insecure about the ideas I had. While not every single one was a winner, I was pretty sure a few were solid, some very good. Still, when I pitched* them, I was met with various levels of no. I let those denials make me think my idea wasn't any good, or that I just didn't know what a good commercial idea was. Or that my writing wasn't good enough. I questioned my own instincts.

But I didn't stop writing. And one day while I was trying to piece together a story, I was surprised by a completely different idea that sprang from my own experience. It sprang practically full-blown. I wrote it out in one burst of inspiration (I'm not saying inspiration doesn't happen; I'm just saying it isn't always available to you), three hand-written pages of what essentially remained the story through all its incarnations. Without going into too much detail, it was about a once-close family torn apart by a secret, a positive look at death and dying way before anyone wanted to think about that. I tried pitching it, but the summary really wasn't the story. So I wrote it. It was optioned as a television movie. It was not made. Then I sold it as a half-hour episode to a syndicated television show. Not the spectacular success I'd hoped for, but the essence of my story remained intact.

And once I'd written something that meant so much to me, I couldn't go back to just coming up with stories that fit a particular demographic but that I wasn't deeply connected to.

I tried, however, because I thought that's what it meant to be a writer. More pitches, more meetings. More frustration.

Meanwhile, I'd started keeping a separate notebook in which I wrote scenes, ideas, character sketches, bits of dialogue that wouldn't get me work in Hollywood, but that I needed to give voice to.

And that were fun to write. And that took up more and more of my time and energy as I gave myself permission to write whatever I really felt like writing. And that eventually became my first novel.

---

* In a "pitch," a writer tells her story idea to someone. That someone could be an agent, manager, film or television executive, director—i.e., a person she is trying to interest in her idea.

I had finally found the stories I wanted to tell once I freed myself from thinking I had to tell a certain kind of story.

I honestly can't remember how I arrived at my death and dying idea. I didn't consciously say I wanted to write that story. Some of my subsequent novels and screenplays began with random snippets that came to me: a character's name, or a situation, once even a title. By then I'd found my subject matter and could run with whatever form an idea took. But I do know that if I hadn't trained myself to sit down to write for a certain amount of time every day, none of it would have happened. Ever. Once I knew the kinds of stories I wanted to tell, it was a matter of showing up and getting to work.

Remember, this is my trajectory. Yours may, or will be, or has been, markedly different. The important message here is this: Your connection to your stories will keep you interested in them. And that's what will keep your audience interested. If your stories aren't keeping you up at night, they won't do that for us, either.

You need to trust your instincts. If you're submitting work professionally, just because someone doesn't want to buy/publish/produce your idea doesn't mean it isn't a fine idea. As discouraging as rejection is, just keep writing.

This is where having a practice pays off. Sometimes I didn't feel like writing this book. Like even now as I type this, I feel like I'm just babbling on, who's going to want to read it, why am I even bothering. I could be cleaning my study, reading something that's already been written by someone else, rearranging my Netflix queue. And yet here I am, slogging away, because somewhere in my brain or body, ingrained in my muscle memory, I know that this is the only way to get to what it is that I have to say.

🚩 **The lesson: Only you know the story you need to tell. And sometimes you have to write it so that other people agree that you needed to.**

6
TAKE RISKS

My screenwriting students will sometimes pitch two script ideas before declaring which to write for the course. Often one of those is what they'll call "out of their comfort zone" because they've been writing horror or action or some genre they love. But this departure idea usually is of a personal nature, based on something that happened to them or to someone in their family.

When I first started writing, I used to jump up from my desk when I had an idea that scared me. Of course I didn't identify it as fear at the time, but that's what it was. I told myself that I needed time to let this idea percolate. I'd tidy up around the house, play with the dog, get something to eat. Of course, by the time I got back to my desk, the idea would be gone.

A writer friend of mine said that if her palms didn't sweat when she was writing, she wasn't taking risks, which meant she wasn't writing what she knew she needed to write.

What was I so afraid of? Revealing a secret? Writing something so personal a reader would assume everything a character did was something I'd done? Fear be damned. I never had to show what I wrote to anyone. I taught myself to sit and write it out. Those scary ideas are often the ones most worth pursuing, the ones that will lead you to the stories you most need to tell. And those will be the stories your audience connects with most fully.

So when students tell me one of their ideas is out of their comfort zone, I encourage them to pick that one. The one that's a little scary, that makes them a little uncomfortable. I encourage them to write what they're afraid to write because that's possibly the first time they'll be deeply connected to their subject matter. And it's scary because who knows what's going to come out when that happens. And because once they've experienced that, and survived (and they all survive), it will change their storytelling forever.

🔖 **The lesson: Don't let a little fear stop you.**

SPEAKER AND MEDIA RESPONSES

The following speaker and media response exercises are designed to make you more comfortable getting out of your comfort zone. I've included them here, but really you could do them any time, string them out as you work on your current project, or make it a part of your routine, your responsibility, even, to keep current with what's out there.

The Speaker Response will show you how other storytellers have had to face their own fears. The Media Response encourages you to look at different kinds of storytelling.

EXERCISE | SPEAKER RESPONSE

Attend at least four lectures, poetry or prose readings. Your local library probably has a bunch of activities that would be excellent for our purpose. Live and in person is preferable, but if that isn't possible, or if you can't find anything in your area, look online.

After each one, write your response to the event. Why you chose this person, how s/he relates to the stories you hope to tell, or to the effect you hope your stories will have on others. Or, if they appear to have no relation to your work or the stories you want to tell, what drew you to this event? Were you able to find some connection that relates to your own stories? What did you learn from the event? What engaged you most? How did the speaker tell his or her story?

Why: I assign responses to my students only partly because I want to make sure they've read the book or attended the event I've assigned. Their responses are valuable beyond bureaucratic academic reasons.

Storytellers don't work in a vacuum. We can find inspiration wherever we go. Being able to articulate what you liked/didn't like about a story will help strengthen your critical ear and eye when you turn it back to your own stories.

You could also consider this a way to find story ideas, get inspiration to bring back to your own work, see how other people tell stories, hear about someone else's process. When you're listening to these people, or even reading interviews with storytellers, look for what they have to say about their experience with their own inner critic. How do they out-write/out-think/outrun it? Their struggles may not be the exact same ones you face, but trust me, they've had them. See what you have in common with someone at the top of their game, or on their way there. How do they use what some might consider their weaknesses to their advantage? How does fear or procrastination drive them to find more creative ways to work?

🔖 **One caveat: Learn from other storytellers, but don't compare your work to theirs. They do their work, you do yours. Only you can tell your story.**

EXERCISE | FIVE MEDIA RESPONSES

These exercises ask you to examine how stories are told in different media and to think about how this relates to your own storytelling. At the very least, you'll get to take a close look at stories in forms you may be familiar with but haven't considered in relation to your own work. I encourage you to move out of your comfort zone for this, to examine new and emerging forms.

I limited this to five areas, but suggest you to explore others on your own. For example, genres you don't usually read/watch/play, book series, graphic novels, manga, web series, hyperfiction, narrative websites, alternate reality games (ARGs), virtual reality.

1. TV show extras: If you've never explored this content for TV series you watch, choose a current television show that you're familiar with, go to its Website, and engage with all its content. This may include but not be limited to: games, character blogs or vlogs, behind the scenes interviews, Twitter and Facebook feeds. Does content differ across the various options for engagement? Is the tone the same? Quality of the content? Write about how this affects your experience of the series.

2. Narrative video game: Play a narrative video game of your choosing for no fewer than five hours (doesn't have to be in one sitting). You do not have to finish or beat the game. After briefly summarizing the game, write about how you experienced its story. How were plot and characters revealed? How is the player involved in the narrative? Did you take time to explore the world, or did you immediately set out on missions? Did you engage with this story differently than you would have with a book, movie, or other immersive narrative? If you're a non-gamer, you might prevail on a gamer acquaintance or relative to play while you watch. I encourage you to take the controller at least once.

3. Art or socially responsible video games: Not all video games are big-budget, multihour extravaganzas. Many smaller games exist that challenge us to think differently about our own lives, about social and political issues. Some aim to educate us. If you're familiar with any art or socially responsible or educational games, feel free to play them for this exercise. If not, here are some sites to explore:

- Molleindustria

- Games for Change

- You can search out other independent games on your own.
  Here are four to get you started: *Braid; Gone Home; Limbo; Never Alone*.

- You might be interested in reading about Twine, an open-source tool for telling interactive, nonlinear stories.

Once you've explored various options, play three or more games and write about your experience. If you generally play more mainstream, commercial games, compare the experience.

4. Screen adaptation: Choose an adaptation that you like. You may pick a film or television show adapted from another medium (a novel, short story, graphic novel, or a Broadway show). Briefly summarize the original story, and list as many changes you can think of that were made in bringing it to the screen. For example, was the story simplified for a film, expanded for a television series, characters added or combined, locations changed? What was gained in the translation from one medium to another? Lost? Did you like one better than the other?

5. Transmedia storytelling: First off, a word about transmedia. It involves a story told across a number of media platforms. (Think *Star Wars, Avatar, Halo*.) Unlike an adaptation, it isn't merely taking the same story that originated as a novel, say, and turning it into a film. It is creating different stories from that original story world that audiences can access and engage with in multiple ways, each story enriching the audience's understanding of that world. So much so that fans contribute their own stories to the world through fan fiction.

Explore a story world you're familiar with or one that is new to you. Try to explore as many layers of the world as possible. This could include film, television, web series, comics, games, toys and trinkets (notepads, pens, key chains, t-shirts, any kind of branded merchandise), books, fan fiction, websites and wikis, theme park rides or entire theme parks, even breakfast cereal. How does each medium tell their stories? Do they all enrich the whole world? If so, how? Which do you engage with most readily? What does the accumulation of details gleaned from various media do for your understanding of or engagement with the story world? Can you think of a story you would create for this world?

Why: It's good every so often to step out of your comfort zone, or to think about what you already read/watch/play, and write your responses in your story notebook. Your story might benefit from being told in a different format. There are lots of ways to tell a story.

7
IT'S ALL IN THE DETAILS

Flannery O'Connor wrote that if someone asks you what your story's about, the only thing to do is to read them the story. She means that it's impossible to separate the parts from the whole—everything in the story has a purpose, and you can't really get the full flavor, meaning, or intention of the story by simply summarizing its plot.

I suppose you could be a wiseass if someone asks you what your story's about and answer, "About eighteen pages," before politely suggesting that they read it.

Or, since you don't want to alienate your audience, you could compose a brief description to rattle off on these occasions. While this by no means is a substitute for the whole piece, writing it can be an excellent exercise in discovering for yourself the gist of your story. One assignment I give at midterm in my advanced screenwriting classes is to write a query letter asking an agent or producer to read the script being written. The purpose of this letter is to introduce yourself and your story, pique the reader's interest in just a few sentences. (In real life, you wouldn't send out a query letter until you'd actually finished your script, book, etc., but writing one is part of the learning process.) I used to require this at the end of the semester, but I noticed an interesting phenomenon: the discrepancy between a student's summary of what her script's about and the class's understanding of it based on the pages we'd been reading all semester. Having students write this letter earlier gives them the opportunity to see where they may have gone off course from their original intentions, or even that their story has changed since they originally conceived it. It's also a good lesson in the fact that we don't work in a vacuum. We may have very definite opinions of what our work is about, but we have no control over how our audience will interpret it.

While composing a brief description can be a helpful tool, a two- or three-sentence logline (a logline is the brief description you read in the TV listings of your newspaper) will never substitute for experiencing the whole story—whether that story is read, watched, listened to, or played.

Consider this summary of the film *Star Wars: A New Hope* from Wikipedia:

> Set "a long time ago in a galaxy far, far away," the film follows a group of freedom fighters known as the Rebel Alliance as they plot to destroy the powerful Death Star space station, a devastating weapon created by the evil Galactic Empire. This conflict disrupts the isolated life of farmboy Luke Skywalker when he inadvertently acquires the droids carrying the stolen plans to the Death Star. After the Empire begins a cruel and destructive search for the droids, Skywalker decides to accompany Jedi Knight Obi-Wan Kenobi on a daring mission to rescue the owner of the droids, rebel leader Princess Leia, and save the galaxy.

Yawn. Maybe it gives us the overarching plot, but that lifeless summary is devoid of every detail that makes the Star Wars universe one of the most popular story worlds in our galaxy. Does it do one iota of justice to the experience of watching the movie? Does it give you any sense of what that experience is going to look or feel like? Does it bear any resemblance to how you'd tell the story if someone asked you about it?

Most likely not, because you'd start with a detail that stood out for you—possibly from the opening crawl setting up the world and mood of the story, or Princess Leia in distress, or the way the droids walk and talk, the richness of the details used to reveal the world of the story. That description merely tells us what happens, no flavor added.

E.M. Forster differentiated between story and plot. Story, he said in *Aspects of the Novel*, is what happens: "The king died and then the queen died." Plot gives us causality: "The king died and then the queen died of grief." So not just *what* happens next, but *why*.

I agree with O'Connor that it may be truly impossible to separate a story from its elements, but we first have to create those individual elements. Dialogue, description, characters, language, tone. It's the details that give a story life—not just life, but its unique life. To overly simplify, the following films all have father/son themes at their core: *Star Wars, Big Fish, Field of Dreams, The Bicycle Thief, Percy Jackson and the Olympians*. Yet you'd never mistake one for the other.

(I could say here that this is why your connection to your material is so important. It's what's going to differentiate your romantic comedy from mine, your space saga from George Lucas's.)

How does this happen? How can so many of the same basic plot lines give us so many different stories? How many times have you guessed what was going to happen—he's going to get the girl; they're going to rob that bank; the car is going to break down—without spoiling your enjoyment of the story. Maybe you only knew *that* it was going to happen; you didn't know exactly *how*, and you want to know how these particular characters are going to act in this particular situation.

So for our purposes, let's think of a story—any kind of story—as an accumulation of details that immerse the audience in the world of the story. There's the sequence of events, of course—this happens, then this, on and on. But for us to follow, for us to want to constantly know now what? And now what? And what now?!—all of which contribute to the why — the storyteller needs to accumulate a multitude of details, so that when we enter the world of the story we can see, feel, touch, taste, and hear it. Who are the characters? What do they look like? How do they dress, walk, speak? Do they carry or wear an object that defines them? Where are they?

But before we get bogged down in these details, we need to examine something essential to every story: conflict.

EXERCISE | CONFLICT

Conflict can come in many forms. Some are obvious and visible: a person pointing a gun, a ferocious great white shark pursuing a small boat, an iceberg looming in the path of an ocean liner. Others are equally motivating but less visible: social norms, peer pressure, one's conscience. Without conflict, the stakes in your story will be low or non-existent. If your main character doesn't have to struggle, why will we care if he achieves his goal? If we don't root for your protagonist to triumph over all obstacles in her path, where's our investment in your story?

I took an acting class in film school. We did one exercise that has stayed with me all these years. In it, two people were given nondescript dialogue which I don't remember as well as the gist of the exercise, but it went something like this:

Person One: "Hi."

Person Two: "Hi."

Person One: "I have to be going. Bye."

Person Two: "Bye."

We were then told to perform the scene.

You try it. Read the lines out loud. Not much going on. Forget that there's no context for the dialogue—who are these people, where does this take place, why does one of them have to leave. No clues or queues as to how to act this.

Now, take that same exchange but tell Person One they must leave the scene and tell Person Two that they must prevent Person One from leaving.

Okay, so we have motivation. That helps. What helps even more is that Person One's motivation is the exact opposite of Person Two's. *Conflict*! So now if we have to act out this scene, we may still not know who these people are, why they're wherever they are, how well or little they know each other. But at least we've given our actors something to *do*, either leave or prevent the other person from leaving. What has stayed with me from that exercise was what conflict added. If I'm motivated to leave the room, I can go. No big deal. And not too interesting to anyone. *Unless*: I'm motivated to leave the room and someone else is preventing me from doing so. Now I have a problem to solve. How I go about solving it will reveal something about my character. How much pressure I'm under to get out of that room (to catch a plane; to save the bridge from exploding; to reconcile with my beloved before it's too late) will up the ante on my resourcefulness and reveal even more about me. The greater the pressure, the higher the stakes, the more the real me will come out. No time to be nice or polite or stand on ceremony if my goal is to save humanity from destruction.

Whatever kind of tale you're telling, the more conflict you can add, the easier time you'll have constructing your stories. Now your characters will have something to force them to act and to make choices under pressure which will reveal their true selves.

If you already know the story you want to tell: Think about what happens in your story. Where it takes place. The outcome. Can you define the main conflict? List all the possible conflicts in your story.

If you're still looking for the story you want to tell: Save these questions for later and move on to Building a Story/Storyworld. Or, consider a story you're familiar with and examine the conflicts facing its characters.

Why: You can't have a story without conflict. Someone wants something, and something or someone prevents them from getting it. That's conflict in a nutshell.

EXERCISE | BUILDING A STORY/STORY WORLD

If we think about a story as an accumulation of details that 1) makes the audience want to know what happens next and 2) can't be summarized without losing its unique characteristics, how do we gather those details?

We'll adapt the old journalistic three questions "who?/what?/where?" for this exercise. What do you need to tell a story? Not all that much when you get right down to it. Some characters (Who). Props—something for the characters to interact with (What). A location, somewhere for those characters to be (Where).

You can do this exercise on your own. It also works well with a group. We'll divide it into two parts: preparation and construction.

Preparation is simple. In your notebook, make a list of possible characters, each with a brief description.

If you're working on your own, try for at least six. If you can break up your group into smaller groups of two or three people, each group could come up with three characters. You could make these descriptions as brief as "a very energetic old man," "a musician with career-threatening carpal tunnel syndrome."

Props now. Three or four. A well-used laptop computer covered with stickers from local restaurants. Great-grandfather's watch chain. A family photo album.

Next, location. Three or four of these as well. A mosquito-infested bog. An enchanted forest. A supermarket parking lot.

Keep them simple. Keep the story out of the descriptions, meaning, don't set up situations in the locations, or have characters interacting with the props. Save that for when you put it all together.

At some point, transfer each building block to its own piece of paper. When I do this for my class, I use a different color for each category (character, prop, location). Fold the paper so you can't see what's on it. Throw it into a hat, pot, box, any container will do. Or just mix them up in their category right on a tabletop.

Now for the **Construction** phase:

STORY WORKOUT | 27

When you have all your building blocks assembled, pick two characters, one location, one prop.

Construct a story using the prompts you've chosen.

If you want to try a variation of this exercise, assign a theme before choosing your building blocks, then write your story. You could also write different stories using the same theme and prompts. If you're in a group, break into smaller teams and, using the same prompts and themes, write a story. See how the stories vary from group to group. (A note about theme: writer and professor John Gardner called theme a fancy way of articulating a character's main problem. A story can have more than one theme.)

Why: You'll see that you can write on command, produce something that you might not want to offer for publication but that works well enough considering the conditions under which you wrote it.

If you're working in a group, it's a great way to practice the art of collaboration—how to riff on someone else's idea, or present your own, learn when to stand up for those you believe in, and when to let go of others.

You might also find this exercise useful when developing your own stories. Rather than work with arbitrary props or characters, take from your own work in progress. Write a paragraph about your character's favorite possession. Describe his or her favorite place. If you're further along in your story and want to switch it up a little, for a fresh view of these people you've been living with for a while, take your own characters and mix them with different locations and props.

EXERCISE | DISSECTING A STORY

Delving deeper into your media history, choose one book, movie, television show, or video game that you really love and that epitomizes the effect you want your stories to have on your audience. Then:

- Write a summary of the story as if you were describing it to someone.
- Where did you start your summary? Is that where your book/movie/show/game started? If not, what made you start there? What jumped out at you?
- What in particular did you connect with? The relationship between the characters? The action sequences? The locations? The soundtrack? Or...?

- How does the story relate to the kinds of stories you want to tell?
- Many details contributed to your willing suspension of disbelief and/or to your understanding of the story you chose for this exercise. You may focus on one aspect more than another, but at least consider each of the following areas:

Language : If you chose a written story, how does the writer's style affect your immersion in the story?

What about dialogue? How do the characters talk? What might that tell you about their background, class, social status? Think about one or two of the main characters: do they come right out and say what they mean, or do they talk around a subject? Do they sound the same?

What else do you learn from dialogue:

About the plot

About the relationship between characters

About the backstory (what happened before the story started)

Characters: Do you like the characters in your chosen story? If you don't like them, can you still relate to them?

Do you believe how they respond to situations?

Where do they live? Work? (Be specific about their jobs: not just "doctor" but "emergency room doctor" or "neurosurgeon." These choices make a difference, just as where you choose to set your story should make a difference.) What do you learn about their social class or economic standing?

How do they dress? Do they have a favorite possession? Any identifying physical traits? Habits?

What do these and any other details you may have listed tell you about them? And how do these details contribute to your engagement with and understanding of the story?

Visual Elements: List all the visual elements that contributed to your understanding and enjoyment of the story. (On a screen, this could be anything you see in a scene. On a page, how characters and settings are described.)

Where is the story set? How does the location affect the overall story? Could this story take place somewhere else? How would that affect the story?

What about specific locations—a character's house or room, office. Lavishly decorated or Spartan? Anonymous or cluttered with personal objects? Claustrophobic? Dark?

What other visual details gave you information about the characters, plot, backstory? For example: did the use of color or lighting affect your understanding of the story? Or did some element of the setting convey information? For example, in a film, a wall covered with family photos might give you a brief history of the family or reveal something about the relationship between the family members. In a novel, how a character views a landscape could reveal a lot about that character's state of mind.

Why: To help you pinpoint your connection to someone else's story, break it down so you recognize those elements you deem most important and how they drew you in and, combined with all the other story details, contributed to the richness of your experience.

Whether it's about super powers, magic, the past, present, or the here and now—it's this accumulation of detail that immerses us in the world of a story and that keeps us in our willing suspension of disbelief.

EXERCISE | RESEARCH

Research is a handy tool for whatever stage you're at in the creation of your story. While an abundance of information is available to us through the internet in the form of articles, books, videos, blogs, vlogs, statistics, images, here's a concept to consider: talk to real people; if possible, take a walk around a location you're considering using.

The Exercise: Take this opportunity to think about the characters in your story. What professions have you chosen for them? Was this a conscious choice, or did the character spring into your mind fully employed as a (whatever)? What does that job say about your character? If you can, interview someone who has that job. What's a typical day like? What kind of props or equipment do they use? Did they need special training or education? What do they like best/ least about their work? Come up with a minimum of ten questions to ask. Jot notes or record your interview.

If you don't know your story yet, or are still working out who your characters are, make an appointment with someone who works in a field not your own, or a co-worker who does something very different from you, and interview them about their job.

Why: In your stories, you're going to write about what you know in the sense that you'll be writing from your own experience, observations you've made. But more than likely you'll want to venture outside your own personal experience and expertise. Talking to someone about their job/profession/field may give you specialized vocabulary you wouldn't necessarily know, access to situations useful to your story, a chance to discover what details you can incorporate that will make your story more believable. Sometimes you can flat out ask—why might a nurse leave a critical patient's bedside? What equipment would a carpenter always have with him in his truck?

Don't forget the other kind of research—looking up information about something you're not familiar with, reading books, articles, looking at photographs. That will yield the same trove of world-building material.

You can apply this research to locations as well, both on line and in person. A walk in a neighborhood you're using in your story might suggest ideas for situations, characters to populate a scene, even the idea for a new scene.

And, remember, when you're off doing research, this is part of your writing process even if you're not actually sitting down and writing your story.

8
TRUTH VS. FICTION

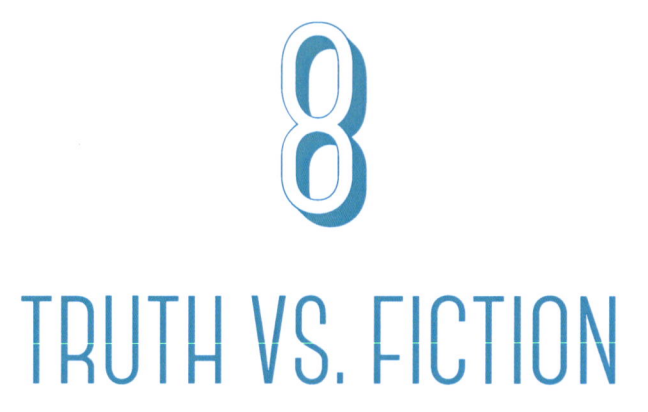

An often repeated scenario in any writing class I've taught goes something like this: workshopping a script or novel excerpt or short story, someone in the class will say, "I didn't believe when X happened." The writer then responds with a defense along the lines of "Well, that's exactly what happened. That's exactly what she said."

Which is precisely the problem. Just because something happened a certain way, or at all, in real life doesn't mean we're going to believe it in a story.

So what's a storyteller to do? How do you accumulate those details so when you drop in your best friend's hysterical or tragic or right-on remark, it works in your story? Because that's where your allegiance lies, to your story, not to the original inspiration for the story.

You want to tell the story of what happened because it affected you so deeply, was so funny, touching, or sad—and you think that if you change it in any way you'll betray some essential element of the event and thus distort its meaning.

Not so.

It's your connection to the event that made you write about it. And it's precisely that connection—not so much the event—that your audience will respond to.

We've all had the I-guess-you-had-to-be-there moment after recounting something that happened that was so funny at the time, really side-splitting, gut-busting, guffawing, one for the books, but our listener just sits there blank-faced, not appreciating the humor, yes?

Do you have a favorite family anecdote, one you've told so many times that it comes out the same? Have you ever told it to someone else who was present at the original event? Someone who says, "That's not how I remember it." But by now your version is set in stone, and has possibly fused in your mind with what actually happened. So much so that it's impossible to unravel what you've constructed from what actually happened. I don't know that it matters. It's all in service to the story.

The goal of our storytelling is to make these events come alive for our audience. By whatever means necessary. By giving your grandfather a better sense of timing than he might have had in life, or adding a punch line to some family story that really never ends; by giving your character three aunts when you really had five, but that's just too unruly for you much less your audience to keep track of so you took the traits you needed and distributed them between these three.

Art reshapes reality. (And I don't just mean painting art—film, literature, television, video games.) Read what artists have said about their work, or about art in general, and you'll find a familiar belief, possibly put best by Picasso who said, and I'm paraphrasing, art is the lie that tells the truth.

What are stories but another kind of truth? A truer truth than what actually happened, a way to make your experience resonate for someone else, to show them that they're not alone in what they're feeling or thinking. Paradoxically, the very specificity of the details you use to tell your story, the more personal and unique, the more an audience will relate to it.

As I said earlier, everything a writer experiences is potential grist for the mill of story.

It doesn't have to be true; you just have to make your audience believe it.

🔖 **The lesson: Fiction, for our purposes, *is* truth.**

EXERCISE | WHAT I HEARD

Part 1: Eavesdrop on at least three conversations and write them down to the best of your ability. You don't have to record them. Just try to capture as much of what you heard as you can. Don't make up anything; don't make people sound smarter or more articulate than they are. Keep the pauses, false starts, etc. For each conversation, make note of who your speakers were, what their relationship was or might have been to the best of your understanding, and where the conversation took place.

Why: To keep your observational skills sharpened. Do people look at each other when they talk? Really focus on the other person?

To train your ear to pick up speech patterns, cadences, regional slang or expressions.

And, of course, to pick up anything that you can use in your own storytelling. To remind you that good story material is all around you.

In my classes, I make a distinction between "conversation" and "dialogue." The first is what we have in real life; the second is what we write for our stories. Dialogue has been shaped by its author, enriched with information that reveals character, backstory, moves the story forward. It is never just people talking—though it should sound just like people talking.

Part 2: Read over what you were able to write down on your eavesdropping forays. Study each conversation. Can you define any basic characteristics of everyday conversation? Did your people speak in complete sentences? Use contractions? Slang? Change topics without any obvious transition? Did the conversation have a definite end, or just trail off or stop abruptly?

What did people's conversations reveal about them? How much information about them, about their lives, could you glean from what you overheard? Did they answer questions directly, or not at all? Try to change the subject? Did family members or spouses or close friends speak in a kind of shorthand that they understood but might not be clear to outsiders?

Conflict is a prime element in fiction. Could you detect any conflict in the conversations you heard?

If you're in a group, read your overheard conversations out loud and discuss the common traits.

Why: Inspiration will fail you. This is the kind of exercise that might come in handy should you get stalled in a project. Getting out into the world to observe raw material never hurt a storyteller. You may even get some great lines for your story, or ideas for scenes or new characters.

EXERCISE | WHAT I SAW

Part 1: After you've kept your story notebook for a few weeks or have a good number of observations from which to choose, whichever comes first, pick one incident or interaction you observed and wrote about—or sketched or photographed or videotaped—to expand into a fictional piece. This must be something you observed directly, not something you read on a page or watched on a screen. You may create a new story, fable, myth, legend, scene, script, or incorporate the observations into a project you've already started.

If you're working in a group, share your stories with each other.

Why: One reason for keeping your story notebook is to have a repository of the details you've accumulated as potential story material you can use. Now is the time to use it. It's also good practice in altering what actually happened in service of your story.

Part 2: Write a one- or two-sentence explanation of why, out of everything you've observed so far, you chose this particular incident. Don't spend more time on Part 2 than on creating your fiction. It's an aid to keep you in touch with your creative process.

Why: What drew you to this observation in the first place? Does it relate to themes you're drawn to? How much did you alter what actually happened? Did you end up with an accurate representation of what happened? Was that what you were going for? Or did you use your original incident as a catalyst for a very different kind of story?

Think about the incidents you didn't choose to fictionalize. What did they have in common, or are you just saving those for later?

This will encourage you to think about the kind of raw material you're interested in and drawn to. It is also an opportunity to examine your creative process: How did you convert that original observation into the fiction you wrote. Don't worry if you can't pinpoint the exact moment of transformation. Again, it's just about being aware.

The moments we observe and/or participate in don't always have a neat or clear resolution. They don't always follow a linear path from beginning to end. People can act out of character—"Funny, she doesn't usually do something like that"—but characters have to be consistent. When we incorporate events from real life into our stories we may have to reshape, mold, adjust them so they add to the accumulation of details that make up our larger story and contribute to the believable fiction we're creating.

Also: If you've lost your momentum, spending a little time writing about writing can help you back into the story. It may help you stay in touch with your practice and identify ways to keep yourself productive.

Have you always kept a notebook or journal? If so, has your story notebook been an extension of that practice, or a new kind of record for you? If this is your first notebook, has it been helpful to you as a storyteller?

If you're in a group, you can use these questions as a springboard for group discussion of the creative process.

9
IT'S NOT ABOUT THE RULES

Somerset Maugham said there are three rules for writing the novel; unfortunately, no one knows what they are.

I've opened writing workshops with that sentence. At "three rules," students grab their pens and notebooks, excited that the class is already paying off with the key to open the locked secrets of their unfinished work. Just follow these three simple rules. Thing is, and what I think Maugham meant, is that novel-writing is just plain hard work and can't be codified or summarized or made any simpler.

For our purposes, for "the novel," substitute the screenplay, stage play, short story, video game, graphic novel, web series, any kind of story you want to tell. And let's pretend those rules are floating out there somewhere, undefined. Why can't we each make our own three rules for writing our stories?

My three could be:

1. Never start writing in the afternoon, especially when you're in the early stages of a project. I've learned over the years that I do everything but write in the afternoon. I can edit, plan my next morning's work, but starting to write later in the day never works for me.

2. Don't overly polish your pages as you write, wait until you've finished the draft. In my first novel, I rewrote and polished each chapter as I went along. So much so that by the time I reached the end of my first draft and needed to make changes to earlier chapters (that's what happens—your story changes as you progress through it), I was so familiar with how the pages read that my revisions stood out to me as if I'd used different colored ink and I couldn't tell if they were an improvement or not.

3. Write faster than your critic yammers in your ear. Mine hovers just above my shoulder and says things like, You're not to going to write that, are you? I've learned to talk back to it as I'm writing: If you think that's bad, wait till you see this! And I keep on typing away.

Those rules may not apply or be helpful to you. Even for me, some days, these three would be more apt:

1. Don't compare yourself to other writers—"good" or "bad"—but only to your own earlier work.

2. Write every day, whether you're inspired to or not.

3. Write some kind of outline, no matter how brief, of the story you're setting out to tell.

So maybe there are five rules. Or ten. Or twelve. Or maybe only one: you have to sit down and just work at it till it's done.

You may want to make up your own rules. Or not. An important part of being a storyteller is learning how *you* do it, what *your* process is. What's the most conducive atmosphere for you to sit down and work: with music, in absolute silence, alone in a room, in a café. Maybe you don't even sit but prefer to stand. And once you get going, how do you get yourself out of a stuck place (I am not a believer in writer's block). Are you able to tell yourself, from past experience, Ah, yes, I always have a hard time right before I'm halfway through. Or, Yes, I come up with excuses not to write when I'm close to finishing a story because I hate saying goodbye to it.

Sidebar here: If you never finish anything, you won't be able to use that experience to help you through the next project. If you're using your notebook to write your first story, make notes of your progress and your lack thereof—yes, that's part of it—your frustrations, minor triumphs, all of it. That information will come in handy when you tackle the next story and the one after that.

Inspiration will fail you. Push through to the end of your story even if you hate it. The real story you need to tell may be lurking just underneath this one, and you have to write off the top layers to get to it. Or this *is* the story you need to tell and you just have to slog through to the end so you can go back and fix it. That's what first drafts are for. That's what revisions are for.

Writing students have a huge advantage here: a teacher telling them when their assignments are due. The rest of us have to make believe (we can do that: we're storytellers!). Give yourself an arbitrary—but realistic (don't set yourself up for failure)—deadline and write to it. A certain number of pages, two scenes, a chapter, to a particular story point, whatever. Just make it concrete so you know when you've reached it and work until you've met that goal. Then move on toward the next one.

You may surprise yourself. You may not produce your favorite pages, but you'll have enough workable material to move forward, and lots to revise. And you'll get better at estimating how slowly or quickly you can finish a chapter, scene, story, which will help you when it's time to set your next deadline.

- Use your notebook to list your own rules.

Why: You can't create your own story following someone else's rules.

10
EVERYONE'S A CRITIC

My first editor gave me the best advice about how to silence the voice that rattles on and on, criticizing what I'm writing. "Write faster than your critic speaks," she told me.

I mentioned earlier that I've learned to talk back to my critic. Maybe that isn't silencing my inner critic so much as learning to ignore what it's telling me, but it works for me. You need to learn how to manage your relationship with the voice that inhibits your creative drive. If you never get anything onto the page (or the screen of your computer or tablet) because you're worried that it isn't going to be perfect or even good enough or exactly what you want it to say, well, then you'll never get anything onto the page. Always err on the side of writing too much. It's easier to cut than it is to look at a few spare sentences and try to figure out what's missing. Once you've read your pages, have at 'em. You can highlight and delete whole paragraphs. It's sometimes fun, or at least cathartic, to slash huge Xs across page after page that you don't want to use. But don't stop yourself before you've even written a word. What's the worst thing that could happen? You could backspace over everything. Never print it and delete the document. Or print it and shred it. You never have show it to anyone. At least get it written, get it out.

When I first started writing, I'd sit at my desk facing bookshelves stuffed with published novels, poetry, short stories. On bad days I'd look at all that writing that had made it into the world and wonder why I bothered. What else was there to say that hadn't already been said by someone else, and better than I'd ever say it? I knew I'd never be as good as those authors.

One day it dawned on me that I never compared myself to people I thought didn't write as well as I did. And finally I realized it didn't matter how good I ever got—that it wasn't as much about the writing as it was about the stories I needed to be telling.

An artist I know puts it this way: she can only compare her work to her own work, not to any other artist's. This is one of her rules. Another one is: Show up and shut up. In other words, get into the studio and get to work. That's all she needs to focus on.

Different people have different relationships to their inner critics. I do my best to ignore mine, though sometimes I need to talk back to it so that I can go on with what I'm writing. Some people listen to theirs. One writer I know views her critic more like a workshop critique partner who's trying to be helpful than a critic bent on tearing apart her stories. So when her critic says, "That's terrible," my friend replies, "I agree 100 per cent. I'll get to work on the rewrite straightaway."

How do you manage your inner critic? Do your best to get to know it and come to an agreement about your working relationship. It's possible to lay ground rules for when to listen to and when to shut out that voice so that you can continue to be productive.

What about external critics? Actual people rather than the nagging voice(s) in your head?

When I send work out into the world, whether it's for critique by friends or editors, or for publication, I make sure it's in the best state I'm capable of creating—not just proofread and spell checked, but revised so many times I couldn't change one more word, not even a comma. I need another person's perspective to see if what I intended to say has made it to the page.

Keep in mind that if you start to show your work to others, or begin submitting work professionally, you will receive comments from many different people, often completely contradictory. To prepare for that, to learn how to distinguish helpful notes from the less helpful, you must trust your instincts and inner voice, know what to take in, what to let go. Trust yourself. And: if more than one person has trouble with the same thing in your story—whether it's a character, stretch of dialogue, description, some of the situations, whatever—it doesn't mean you need to cut those bits. You do, however, need to accept that you may have failed to convey your original intention. You will need to go back to your work and see how to get what you wanted onto the page. Take their notes seriously, but also with a grain of salt.

Here's the thing: people are going to have all sorts of opinions about your work. And their own agendas, known or unknown to you. Sometimes people give notes on how they would have written the story, or based on something that just happened to them. Sometimes their notes come out of left field. Or outer space. That's why the grain of salt.

You need to learn to take in what's useful to you, discard the rest.

That becomes easier with time. Especially if you've trusted your instincts, taken risks, followed your own rules and creative process, and told the story you needed to tell.

Which is what I've tried to do here.

11
CONCLUSION

Well, actually you're going to come to your own conclusions in these final exercises.

EXERCISE | "ONE" PROJECT

Create one original story.

I assign this as a final project in my Story class. I do not give my students any more guidelines than this, other than to say each will have up to ten minutes to present their story to the class, and that they must turn in a written description of their project. Since they have the opportunity to meet with me in person if they have questions, I will tell you that over the semesters students have produced for this assignment: a tarot reading; a flash animation creation myth; a one-page cartoon about existentialism; an illustrated hero's journey cycle; poems; photo essays; songs; a step dance; an original monologue; short films. That's only a small sample to give you the range of possibilities.

Any story. Any way you want to present it.

You have tremendous leeway here. You could be traditional (a photo, as long as it tells a story; a poem; a fable, contemporary legend or myth); or not.

If you're working in a group, you might want to consider specific guidelines regarding length or due dates for each person's project. If you're on your own, set yourself a realistic deadline for finishing your story.

Why: Isn't this why you bought the book?

EXERCISE | STORY (RE)DEFINED

For many years I thought Kurt Vonnegut had defined story thus: ?!

I don't remember where or when I first read this. But I've had that definition in my head for so long that when a student did some research and found that Vonnegut had actually defined it as a question mark, an exclamation point, and a period, and said these were the outline of a three-act story, I was faced with a dilemma: whether or not to be true to Vonnegut's definition.

As a screenwriter and teacher of the craft, I know a lot about three-act structure. I've got nothing against it as you know from reading earlier in this book. (I also like filmmaker Jean-Luc Godard's opinion that every story should have a beginning, middle, and end—not necessarily in that order.) But I've thought of the definition as ?! for so long that if I add that period, the meaning feels too final and confining.

So for this exercise, let's define story as: ?!

What does that definition mean to you? How does it relate to the stories you want to tell?

Why: This is an opportunity to reflect on what you think is the essence of a story, as well as on your relationship to the stories you want to tell, on how stories affect you, on how you want your stories to affect your audience—to define, or to redefine, story for yourself.

You could use it to look back at what you've completed and forward to what you want to work on next.

EXERCISE | GOALS REVISITED

If you've made it this far, Congratulations! If you achieved your original goal, good for you! If you've arrived here having switched/adjusted/amended your original goal, Yay!

Look back at the creative goal you set for yourself. Did you accomplish it?

If so, how does that make you feel?

If not, did something keep you from achieving your goal, or did your goal change as you progressed through the exercises?

If your goal changed, describe how it changed and what you learned from that adjustment.

Why: The better you understand your process, the more honest you are about your routines and rituals, the more productive you will be with your storytelling practice. As I said early on, the more realistic you make your goal, the easier time you will have achieving it.

If you didn't hit your mark the first time, take a look at the possible reasons. Too ambitious? Not realistic? Be as honest as you can about what kept you from achieving your goal. What strategies might you develop to prevent that from happening in the future?

If your goal changed—your story turned out to be something other than you'd expected, and you needed more time, less time, more research, whatever. No worries.

This is all progress. Storytelling is a wonderfully messy business. Your minor character suddenly turns out to have a bigger personality than you thought and takes on a greater role. Or the story you thought you were telling turns out to be merely the introduction to the story that you really needed to tell. Your story will surprise you and move you (and sometimes itself) in ways you may not have expected. This is a good thing. It means it will do the same for your audience.

A goal is something to aim for. It isn't set in stone. Especially if you've imposed it for yourself. An external professional deadline is a different matter, but even there you can work backwards from your final due date to create intermediary deadlines for yourself. A deadline can be just another way to give some structure to your process, especially as you learn more about your habits and the pace at which you work.

12
THE END

I moved to Los Angeles thinking of myself as a director and became a writer. But it took me a very long time to call myself a Writer. If I'd met you in those early days and you asked what I did, I would say, "I'm a writer." Followed immediately by a qualifier to let you know that you wouldn't have read anything I'd written, I hadn't sold anything. I might have been able to say it, but I wasn't entirely convinced of it because I hadn't yet been "successful."

When I lived in Los Angeles I was a full-time writer and a part-time teacher of writing. Then I moved to Ithaca, New York, and became a full-time teacher and a part-time writer. While I was looking for work in Ithaca, I was also trying to begin my fourth novel. When I started teaching, I had to put it aside. At first, that was a very difficult transition for me. I agonized about losing my identity as a Writer. I agonized at not being able to write. But I simply couldn't manage my new teaching schedule and my former writing schedule simultaneously.

One day, I had the following progression of thoughts: I can't keep this up. I can't manage teaching and get any kind of momentum on my writing. I'll never get this novel written. I'll never get anything written. I'll never write another book.

That stopped me in my tracks.

What if I never wrote another book or screenplay?

What if?

I thought about that.

And I confess, there was something very liberating about the notion of never writing again. I'd never have to think of another "original" idea, or grapple with developing characters, writing pages of backstory that would never make it into the finished piece, nor have to toil away at revision after revision. I wouldn't even have to get started. I could take a walk by myself, no cast of characters trailing along. I had gainful employment, was a responsible member of society. I didn't need to have this other job.

To be honest, I felt kind of relieved.

I came to accept myself as someone who used to be a Writer, and I dove into my teaching with renewed gusto.

Then one day, out of nowhere, I had an idea for a story. Not just a passing thought, but an idea that hit me so hard I had to write it down. And then expand. And then tweak a little. And expand some more.

Though I never made a conscious decision to do so, I was writing again.

Some of what I wrote I published. Not everything. But that wasn't the only reason I wrote. Don't get me wrong. I want an audience. But as much as I hoped—hope—someone would read them, I needed to be telling myself those stories, living with those characters, creating those worlds.

What I had learned was: I cannot not write. Whatever else I do, I am a Writer.

Endings are hard. I often get an idea for my next project when I'm finishing up the one I'm working on. I think that's my way of easing the pain of saying goodbye to the world and characters I've created, allaying my fear that I'll never come up with another idea again.

That's the beauty of being a storyteller—once you've finished creating one story, you can go on to start another. Maybe it's a sequel and you get to spend more time in the world you've created. Or it's a different genre entirely. Or maybe you've told the one and only story you've ever wanted to tell and can stop there.

Whatever the case for you, I hope these exercises have given you and your ideas a good workout.

Enjoy your stories. Don't take them for granted. They're a gift to be nurtured.

The End

APPENDIX A

On Constructive Criticism: Giving

Many writers participate in writing groups to share their material, receive and give feedback, talk shop. For them, being in a group eases the isolation of writing, provides an audience for new material, or fresh eyes on work they're too close to and can no longer be objective about. Belonging to one is not required to be a good writer. But if you're in one—or in a class where you *are* required to share work—you can make the most of it.

To get the most out of your group workshop process, remember: Your energetic, astute, and constructive participation in discussion is essential. Everyone in your workshop or writing group owes to everyone else's story a measure of respect and serious attention and creative intellectual engagement. Do not underestimate the value of giving notes to and receiving notes from other storytellers.

Before opening the discussion of someone's story, set ground rules. You might want to set a specific page length, or a time limit for each discussion. Depending on the size of your group and its dynamics, you might consider timing each person's individual response as well.

When discussing someone else's work:

The more you are able to be objective about what works and what doesn't work—and why—in a story, the more you will be able to call on that objectivity when you look at your own writing.

Critiquing other writers' pages will sharpen your critical eye/ear and train you to catch mistakes or unclear parts you might miss in your own work because you're too close to it. (When you write, it helps to read your pages out loud.)

Reading someone else's work-in-progress will also let you see how others solve problems you might be having in your own story.

Make your comments helpful. You're not in competition with the others in your group.

Be truthful and considerate; the writer will have spent a great deal of time on the work and deserves a generous response.

Comment on what's written, not what you would have written. It's not your job to re-write someone's pages, merely to comment on what took you out of the story.

If you don't understand something, ask about it. This will help the writer, who might think something's clear when it isn't.

When you comment on someone's story, tell them what you liked about it. Also tell them if something didn't work for you. Perhaps the dialogue was weak, or descriptions overly long or repetitive. What took you out of the story? Made you lose interest? Was something not clear to you? Did you believe the story? The characters? Your comments should be very specific. You are trying to help the writer, and even critical comments, especially when supported by specific examples, will do that.

If someone in the group has made the same comment you were planning to make, briefly mention that, then give the writer something new to note. There's also no need to point out typos and spelling errors—you should mark those directly on the pages. Though by all means tell the writer if lack of proofreading or numerous grammatical errors distracted you.

And remember: Make your group/workshop/class a safe place. Comments are about the story being discussed, not about the writer.

APPENDIX B

On Constructive Criticism: Receiving

When you begin submitting work professionally, or if you workshop projects in a writer's group, class, or workshop, you will receive comments from many different people, often completely contradictory. Part of your practice will be to learn to trust your instincts and inner voice, know what comments to take in, which to let go of.

To prepare for that, you need to learn how to distinguish helpful notes from the less helpful. Sometimes that's a question of practice, listening to how people respond to others in your group and measuring their responses against your own. Whose opinions always match yours? Or, if they differ, still strike you as reasoned and articulate and genuine? This may be someone whose notes you want to give credence to versus someone whose critiques of others you almost always disagree with, or that seem ill-considered or off-base. As you find people whose opinions you value, you'll find that even a less than totally positive response to your work can be of use to you.

When your work is being discussed:

YOU WILL NOT SPEAK. This forces you to listen to what is being said. You do not need to defend your work.

That first point bears repeating: You do not need to defend your work. Getting your group to understand why you wrote something the way you did will not make you a better writer. Making it work on the page will.

Almost any critique can be helpful, especially if you're not defensive.

If more than one person has trouble with the same thing in your story—whether it's a character, stretch of dialogue, description, some of the situations, whatever—it doesn't mean you need to cut those bits. You do, however, need to accept that you may have failed to convey your original intention. Something took your audience out of the story. Whether or not you agree with their explanation of why it did, or what you should do to fix it (see Appendix A: On Constructive Criticism/ Giving), what's important to note is that something took them out of the story. You will need to go back to your work and see how to get what you wanted onto the page. The oral feedback and the written notes you receive from your group should provide some guidance for you.

After your group has commented on the work, you may ask questions of them. This is to help you clarify issues you might have that did not come up in the discussion, or to clarify something that did come up. But again, you are not to defend the work; you don't need to refute anyone's comments.

After the critique, it is okay to specify particular area(s) you want comments on, such as dialogue, action or description, a certain character, etc.—in addition to the general notes you received.

Made in United States
North Haven, CT
05 January 2024